The Weeping Willow

by Nicole Olsen

Illustrated by Stefani A. Allegretti

Dedicated to those we've lost and those we love and
for those out there who are learning that it's okay to cry.

With appreciation and thanks to
God, the ultimate Artist and Author,
and our family for whom without, we would not be.

One day, a bird visited
a weeping willow tree,
And as she was hopping
from branch to branch,
the bird could see
The tree begin to cry,
and as she cried the bird,
Asked "Why"?
At the risk of sounding absurd
the willow answered.

"I cry every day,
and every which way,
up, down,
all around,
tears they just come and visit me."

The bird was confused
and felt sad for the willow.
"Why?
Why must you cry every day?"

"I don't know really,
If there is something wrong.
I think it's just a letting go
Of a particular song
To share the inside with the outside maybe
A way for me to be lately."

And the bird wanted to help.
"Oh you don't want to cry in public though.
And make sure you use a tissue
you don't want others thinking you have an issue.
And make sure you smile after,
So others know you are okay
And make sure you have a reason
Or you can say it's just the season."

"What if I just want to cry?
For no reason at all?
What if it's a way to say good bye
To yesterday,
To the moment in time that's now,
To the questions of how
The beauty in the world happens
Every day,
What if I'm just sad,
For sadness sake,
Should I hold it in then?
Should I stop the tears
again and again?"

"It scares me so.
It makes me just want to get up and go.
To leave this place of uncertainty
To fly and never look back
Like there is some emergency."

"Well you have to do what you have to do
and feel what you have to feel, I know
but for a moment direct your attention
away from the emotional throws.
There is something deeper you'll find,
Something deeper, maybe divine,

A place inside you where you can see
Sadness for who she really is,
A beautiful place inside
To get to know,
Not to fly from and hide,
She'll help you, she'll be there,
So that peace may abide.

She may even help you to see,
And you may finally understand,
How sadness can really a friend, come to be."

"Well, now that you put it that way,
I don't really know,
I suppose it's okay to show
Sadness and tears,
Maybe it's just one of my fears,
To cry in front of others
And to show sadness."

And the willow continued,
"I cry
and every which way,
up, down,
all around,
tears they just come and visit me."

"I cry
Because I realize
That the real stuff of life
Was nothing what I thought it was
When I was a sprout.
It's the passage of time,
The babies born,
Who will one day leave their nest,
Watching the sun rise everyday
And set in the west,"

Watching a bird work all day
And finally take time to rest.
Watching the hard work
That it takes To make a nest.
It's the people you love,
And the memories of old,
And the new beginnings
And the hardships
And the happy times,
And the sad times,
And the wishes and the dreams
It's all so mystical and wonderful
It seems.
And I'm very old,
Maybe a hundred years fold.

In a single tear,
There are so many words.
So I cry to get them out
I suppose,
To share the words
Without speaking them,
to share the compassion
for the fears while feeling them,
to share the inside with the outside."

And the bird understood,
and finally felt sadness.
"That makes a lot of sense to me.
Please excuse the tears
That now you see."

"Don't worry, my friend.
It's natural,
A random sort of magical
Where the inside meets the outside.
The tears and the fears
And the sadness will pass,
Just wait a moment
And let the tears amass,
They will come,
And now let them go.
And remember,
I'm your friend,
I'm here for you,
No judgment, no depends,
it is okay to feel,
it's just a part of being real."

The bird saw what the willow saw,
And was grateful.
"I seem to have found a new way to be,
A new way to see,
And it's all thanks to you,
I see now that sadness is not
Something to hide,
But a real part of being
On this life's ride.
Just like joy and happiness,
Sadness needs her time too,
It's part of being whole.
It is okay to feel,
It's just a part of being real.

The laughter and joy will come again,
Just wait and trust
But sadness,
She is a must,
If I am to truly enjoy
happiness again."

And the bird learned
a lot that day
And if tears wanted to come,
they may,
because she knew
that all feelings
belong.

From then on she would visit the willow,
And sometimes her song
Was of happiness and sometimes of sadness
for she knew that it was okay to feel,
it was just a part of being real.

Until next time...

from the Collection of Emotionful Stories

About the Author

Nicole studied Playwriting and Theatre Studies
at Marymount Manhattan College in
New York where she received a Bachelor of Arts degree.
She continued on with her studies and received her Masters Degree
in Oriental Medicine. Nicole practices acupuncture and herbal
medicine at Positive Life Acupuncture inWarwick, NY
and practices and teaches yoga at Vastu Health Center, where she is grateful to
share space with beautiful people who she feels connected to on her soul's journey.
Nicole lives in Upper Greenwood Lake, New Jersey
just next to the Appalachian Mountains with her loving partner,
Martin and their two puppies.
Her inspiration comes from prayer, meditation and the
people she is blessed to experience this life with.
Writing is her way of staying sane and she is grateful to share
it with you, this time around.

About the Illustrator

Stefani A. Allegretti is an educator, freelance writer and
interdisciplinary, contemporary artist specializing in mixed media and
digital art. Stefani received her formal training at the University of Pittsburgh
where she received a Bachelor's degree in Studio Art in 2009. She also holds
a Masters Degree in Education, a Bachelor's degree in English and
multiple certifications. Although Stefani has been creating art since she was a child,
her interest in creating evolved considerably while living on Long Beach Island,
a tiny barrier island situated off of the coast of New Jersey.
It was there that she developed a profound appreciation
for the natural beauty of the coastal environment,
the environment and the natural world in general, which is reflected
in the majority of her work. She is also interested in the
connection between aspects of nature as they relate to the human body and in
exploring the human-to-human connection through the use of various technologies.
For more information, visit www.stefaniallegrettiart.com.